Frank Schaffer Publications®

Published by Ideal School Supply
An imprint of Frank Schaffer Publications
Copyright © 1999 School Specialty Children's Publishing

All Rights Reserved • Printed in China

No part of this publication may be reproduced, stored in a retrieval system, or transmitted, in any form or by any means, electronic, mechanical, photocopying, recording, or otherwise, without the prior written permission of the publisher.

ISBN 1-56451-295-9

Send all inquiries to:
Frank Schaffer Publications
3195 Wilson Drive NW
Grand Rapids, Michigan 49544

Flip-Flash™ Math: Addition & Subtraction Facts

5 6 7 8 9 10 11 12 WKT 10 09 08 07 06 05

Helpful Hints for Learning the Facts

Flip and Check Say the answer to a fact, then flip the page to check.
The answer is the first number on the flip side of the page.

| 4 + 2 = | 6 − 2 = | | 8 − 3 = | 5 + 3 = |
flip   flip

Double Your Power Learn the double-number facts.
Use them to help you remember other facts.

| 1 + 1 = | 2 + 2 = | 10 + 10 = |

Power Up With Turnarounds Learn pairs of "turnaround" facts. If you know one, you know the other one too.

| 1+8= | 8+1= | | 5+10= | 10+5= |

Tackle the Hard Ones Find the facts that give you trouble. Draw a picture to help you "see" the fact in your mind.

6+7=   ○○○○○○
       ○○○○○○○

Make It a Game Make up games to help you recall the facts quickly. Play the games with your friends and family.

Addition Chart

+	1	2	3	4	5	6	7	8	9	10	11	12
1	2	3	4	5	6	7	8	9	10	11	12	13
2	3	4	5	6	7	8	9	10	11	12	13	14
3	4	5	6	7	8	9	10	11	12	13	14	15
4	5	6	7	8	9	10	11	12	13	14	15	16
5	6	7	8	9	10	11	12	13	14	15	16	17
6	7	8	9	10	11	12	13	14	15	16	17	18
7	8	9	10	11	12	13	14	15	16	17	18	19
8	9	10	11	12	13	14	15	16	17	18	19	20
9	10	11	12	13	14	15	16	17	18	19	20	21
10	11	12	13	14	15	16	17	18	19	20	21	22
11	12	13	14	15	16	17	18	19	20	21	22	23
12	13	14	15	16	17	18	19	20	21	22	23	24

$$2-1=$$

$1+2=$

$3-2=$

1+4=

$$5-4=$$

1+6=

7−6=

$1+8=$

$9-8=$

1+10=

11−10=

1+12=

$$13-12=$$

$2+2=$

$4-2=$

$2+3=$

$$5-3=$$

$2+5=$

$7-5=$

$$2+7=$$

$9 - 7 =$

2+9=

11−9=

2+11=

13−11=

3+1=

4-1=

$3+3=$

$6-3=$

$3+4=$

7 − 4 =

$3+6=$

$$9 - 6 =$$

$3+8=$

11−8=

$3+10=$

$13-10=$

$3 + 12 =$

15−12=

4+2=

$6-2=$

4+4=

$$8-4=$$

$4+5=$

$$9-5=$$

4+7=

11-7=

$4+9=$

13 − 9 =

4+11=

15−11=

5+1=

6−1=

$5+3=$

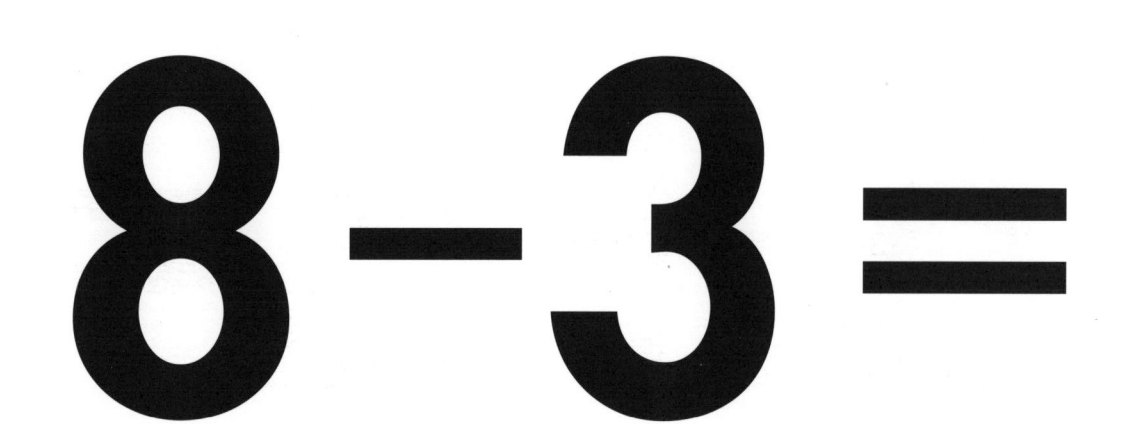

$5+5=$

$$10-5=$$

$5+6=$

11−6=

$5+8=$

$13 - 8 =$

$$5+10=$$

15−10=

$$5+12=$$

17−12=

6 + 2 =

8 − 2 =

$$6+4=$$

10 − 4 =

6+6=

12 − 6 =

$$6+7=$$

13 - 7 =

$6+9=$

$$15-9=$$

$6+11=$

17−11=

7+1=

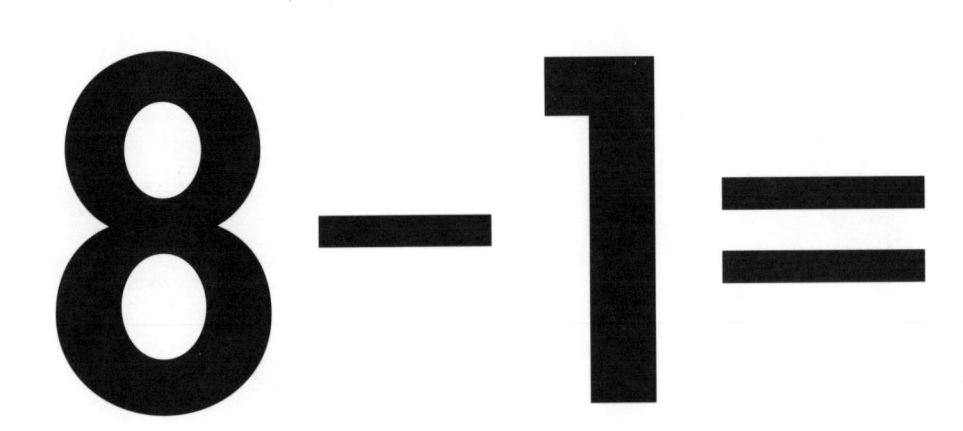

$$7+3=$$

$$10-3=$$

7+5=

$$12-5=$$

$7+7=$

14-7=

$7+8=$

$$15-8=$$

$7+10=$

17-10=

$7+12=$

19−12=

$8+2=$

$$10-2=$$

$$8 + 4 =$$

12 - 4 =

$$8+6=$$

$14 - 6 =$

16 - 8 =

$8 + 9 =$

17 − 9 =

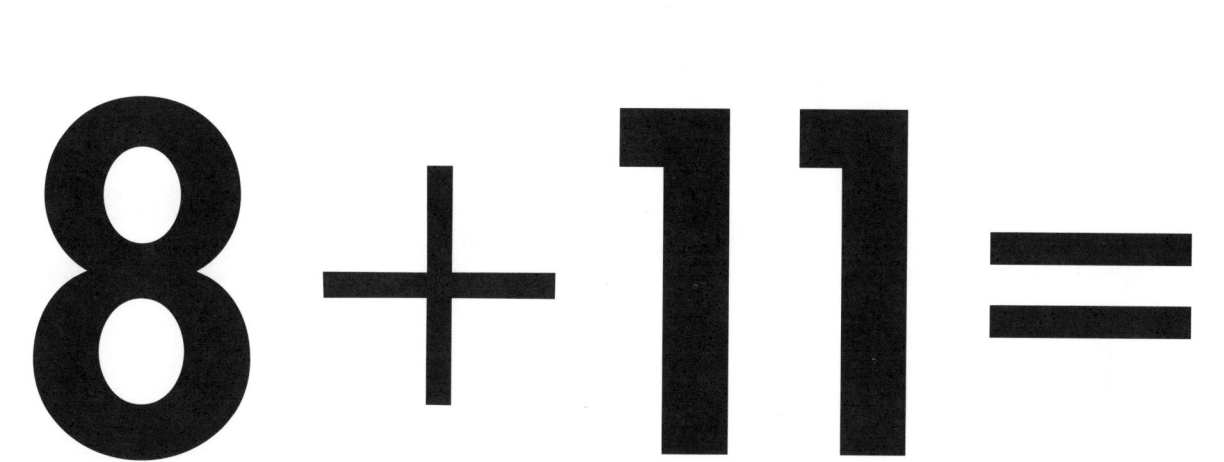

$$19-11=$$

$9+1=$

$$10-1=$$

$9+3=$

12−3=

$$9+5=$$

14-5=

9+7=

$$16-7=$$

$9+9=$

18-9=

9+10=

19−10=

9+12=

$$21-12=$$

10 + 2 =

12-2=

$$10+4=$$

14 - 4 =

$$10+6=$$

16−6=

$10 + 8 =$

18-8=

$$10+10=$$

20−10=

10+11=

21-11=

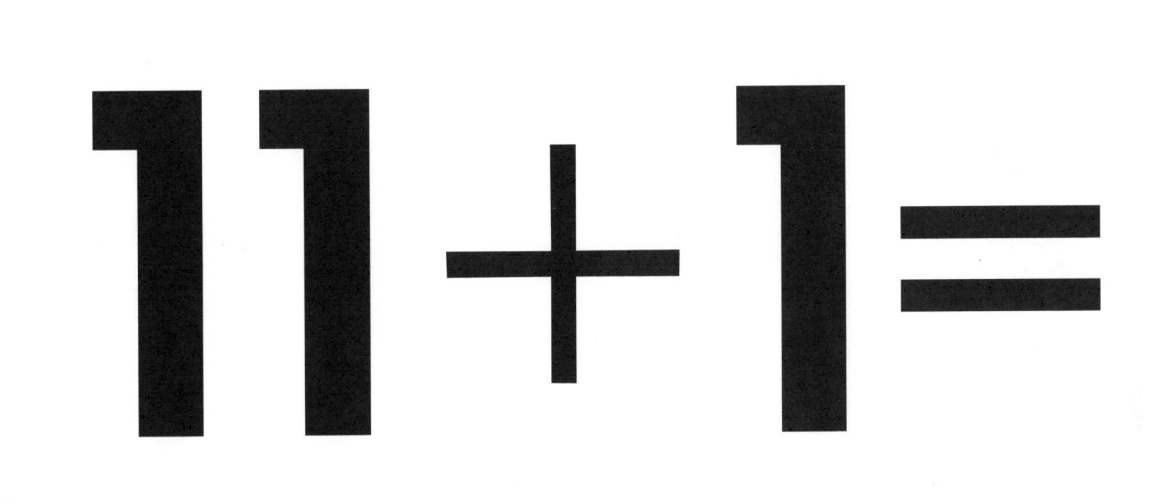

12 − 1 =

$11+3=$

14 − 3 =

$11+5=$

16-5=

$$11+7=$$

$$18-7=$$

11+9=

20−9=

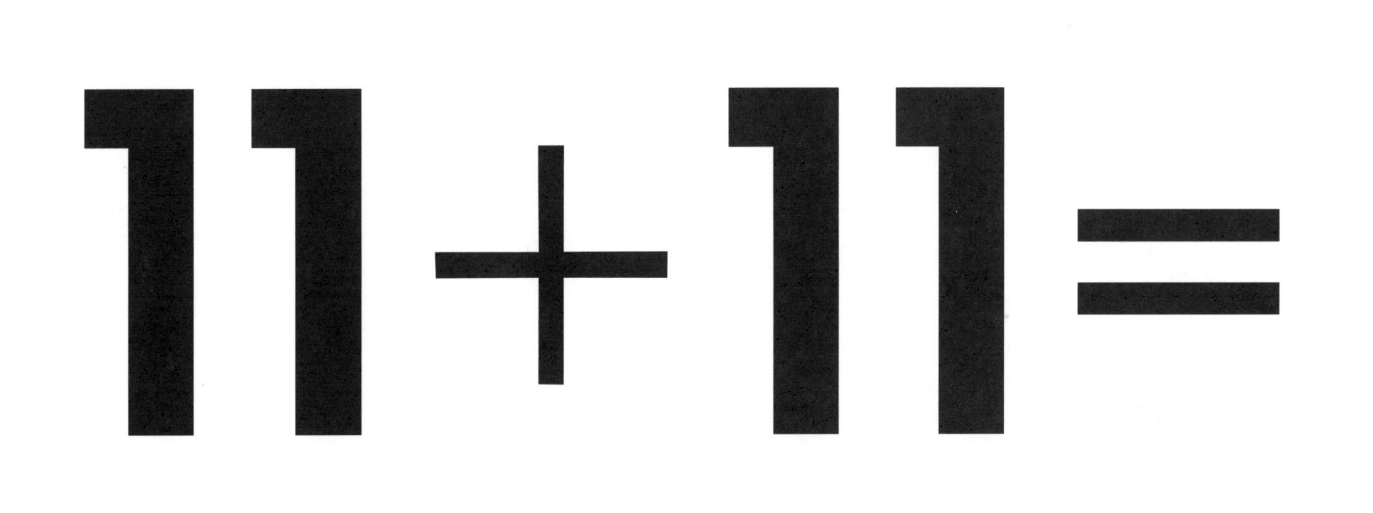

22-11=

11+12=

$$23-12=$$

12+2=

14-2=

12+4=

16 - 4 =

12+6=

$$18-6=$$

12 + 8 =

20 − 8 =

$12+10=$

22-10=

$$12+12=$$

24-12=